THE BRITISH AND THE MAYA

WITHDRAWN FROM STOCK

Frontispiece:
Water-colour painting by Adela Breton
of an atlantean figure from the site of
Chichén Itzá, Yucatán.
(City Museum, Bristol)

THE BRITISH AND THE MAYA

Elizabeth Carmichael

Published by the Trustees of the British Museum
London 1973

Acknowledgements

Prepared by the Ethnography
Department at the Museum of
Mankind 6 Burlington Gardens
London WIX 2EX

My thanks are due to those who helped with this booklet by providing, and allowing to be used, material and information: to the Director and staff of the Bristol City Museum for making available and lending material on Adela Breton and to David Collison of BBC TV for his help in obtaining photographs. Plates 5 and 6 are reproduced by courtesy of the Société de Géographie, Paris; Plates 9 and 10, by courtesy of the Museum of the American Indian, Heye Foundation, New York; and Plate 12 by courtesy of the Smithsonian Institution, National Anthropological Archives, Washington DC. Giles G Healey gave permission for the use of his photograph of Eric Thompson on the cover and Mrs R H Shepard likewise for the portrait of Juan Galindo on page 14.

Adrian Digby and Norman Hammond have both helped with their sections and I thank Ian Graham for reading and commenting upon the entire manuscript. I am especially grateful to J Eric S Thompson who, in addition to reading the manuscript, has throughout its writing given invaluable aid and encouragement.

Contents

List of plates

Map of Mexico, Guatemala and adjacent countries. The shaded area indicates the Maya area shown in the detailed map overleaf.

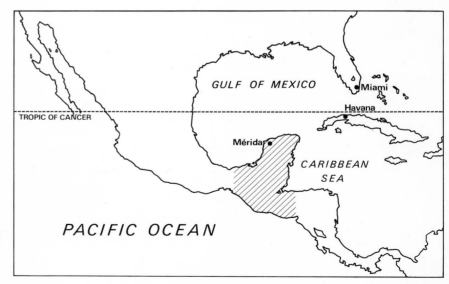

GULF OF MEXICO

Miami

TROPIC OF CANCER

Havana

Mérida

CARIBBEAN SEA

PACIFIC OCEAN

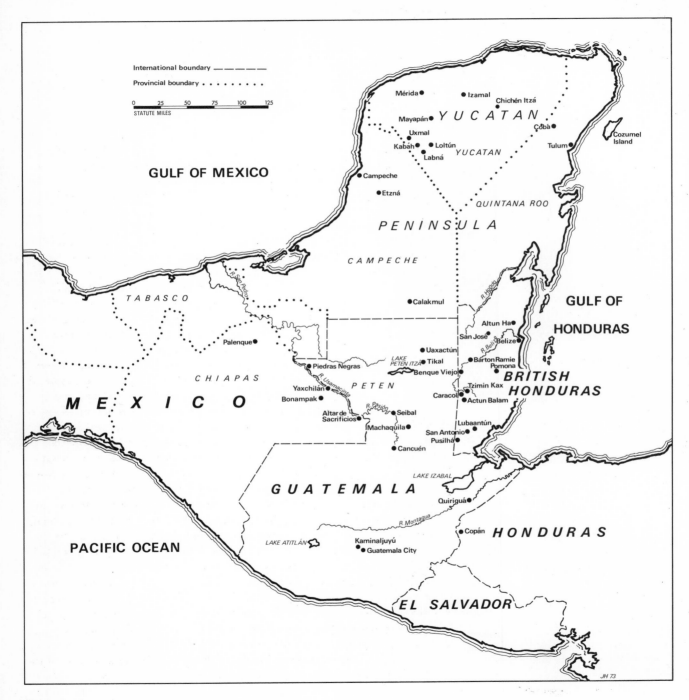

International boundary ── ── ──
Provincial boundary · · · · · · · ·

0 25 50 75 100 125
STATUTE MILES

GULF OF MEXICO

Mérida ●
● Izamal
Chichén Itzá ●
Mayapán ●
Y U C A T A N
Uxmal ●
Kabáh ● ● Loltún
● Labná
YUCATAN
● Cobá
Tulum ●
Cozumel Island

● Campeche
● Etzná

QUINTANA ROO

P E N I N S U L A

C A M P E C H E

R. San Pedro

T A B A S C O

GULF OF
HONDURAS

● Calakmul

Palenque ●

R. Hondo

Altun Ha ●
San Jose ●
Belize ●
R. Belt

M E X I C O

C H I A P A S

● Piedras Negras

LAKE PETEN ITZÁ
Uaxactún ●
Tikal ●
Bárton Ramie ●
Pomona
Benque Viejo ●

R. Usamacinta
P E T E N

BRITISH
HONDURAS

Yaxchilán ●
Bonampak ●
Altar de Sacrificios ●
R. Pasión
● Seibal
● Machaquila
● Cancuén

Tzimin Kax ●
Caracol ●
● Actun Balam
● Lubaantún
San Antonio ●
Pusilhá ●

LAKE IZABAL

G U A T E M A L A
● Quiriguá

R. Montagua

● Copán H O N D U R A S

LAKE ATITLÁN
Kaminaljuyú ●
● Guatemala City

PACIFIC OCEAN

E L   S A L V A D O R

JH 73

8

Introduction

The Pre-Columbian civilizations of Middle America seem to share certain basic traits, possibly arising from the sharing (in Michael Coe's words) of a 'common cultural origin, so far back in time that it may never be brought to light by archaeology'. Of these traits, certain were developed in a highly distinctive manner by the peoples living in the area now covered by the most westerly parts of Honduras and El Salvador, Guatemala, British Honduras and parts of the Mexican states of Tabasco and Chiapas, Campeche, Quintana Roo and Yucatan. This was the vast area in which, during the fifteen centuries preceding the Spanish conquest, Maya civilization developed. With the Maya the preoccupation with time common to all Middle American peoples was evolved to an extraordinary degree of refinement. Correspondingly the hieroglyphic writing used in the recording of their observations attained a form vastly more complex than any others in the Middle American area. The great ceremonial centres of the Maya area with their temples, palaces and plazas achieved an outstanding peak of architectural grandeur. The remains of these can still be seen today and have aroused an intense interest and curiosity ever since the first European traveller set eyes upon them. The soaring temple mounds, the crests of which break through the surrounding jungle, the elaborately carved stelae and the sheer vastness of the area covered by these ruins have inspired many to join the quest for the discovery of new sites and to record their findings, always with the hope of revealing some further fact to help unravel the history of the Maya.

It is not the intention of this exhibition to provide a complete history of exploration and archaeology in the Maya area, but to draw attention to the invaluable contributions made by British travellers and scholars in this field, and to show that this interest is not dead but one actively pursued at the present time. There has never been much encouragement for people living in the British Isles to take up Maya studies. Although the collections of Maya material in museums are adequate, and by diligent search in various libraries most of the background literature can be found, there has been until recently no university teaching of American archaeology and precious little general literature of the right sort readily available to start the student on his way. Perhaps the high quality of the work produced by those few who were enterprising enough to continue in spite of the difficulties is partly at least the product of this adversity.

In preparing this exhibition I have several times set out the portraits of the people represented and tried to recognise some feature that they might have in common. It is, however, a very motley crew and the best common factor I can suggest is that all were tough and resilient, and all enthusiasts. Reading their own accounts of their work where these exist has often made me envious and restless, even when I reflect what hard work it can be to climb to the top of a Maya temple mound that is cleared of vegetation and partially restored. It is now comparatively easy to reach many of the archaeological sites which formerly took days of riding on mule back, wading across rivers and clearing back the jungle (Ian Graham, however, still does just this in the rain forests of the Petén). But the effort involved with its attendant discomforts and hazards never seems to have deterred those who go in search of the Maya.

I am aware that this is not a complete gallery of the British Mayanists. I should like to have included, for example, the descriptions of seventeenth-century Mexico and Guatemala given by Thomas Gage in his *The English-American . . . or, a New Survey of the West Indies* (London, 1648). Fortunately J Eric S Thompson has edited this work in a volume to which I can here refer anyone interested in this early traveller.

Even if only for the name's sake I should have liked Captain John Carmichael to have a place. He is of interest, in fact, as the first person to locate in the mid-nineteenth century the site, later christened Lubaantún by Thomas Gann, where the British Museum carried out excavations under the leadership of Captain Joyce in 1926–7 and to which Norman Hammond returned in 1970. The rather sad tale of Captain Carmichael is given by Gann in his book *Maya Cities*; an account of Carmichael's lecture to the British Association for the Advancement of Science appears in the report of that body for 1870.

I learned too late that as 'a native of the island of Jersey of French parentage' (*Dr Le Plongeon in Yucatan*, Stephen Salisbury Jr, Worcester, 1877) I might have included Dr Augustus Le Plongeon. Perhaps it is better that his on the whole disastrous excavations in the early eighteen-seventies, principally at the site of Chichén Itzá, Yucatán, and his highly eccentric interpretations of Maya art and inscriptions are given only brief mention. Eric Thompson in pointing out my omission recalled that 'Le Plongeon claimed to have proved that the Maya had the electric telegraph and used a metric form of measurement, and that the Greek alphabet was a Maya story of the sinking of Atlantis'. He did however unearth the first sculpture of the type still known as *Chac-mool* (a name he gave to it) at Chichén Itzá, and the photographs of this operation, many of which include Le Plongeon with a waist-length beard or Mrs Le Plongeon in travelling dress with long pantaloons would have added a colourful note to these pages.

Mention should be made of Miss Annie Hunter, the superb draughts-woman who under Alfred Maudslay's supervision produced the drawings for his great archaeological volumes of the *Biologia Centrali-Americana*. I could, however, find scant information concerning her apart from Maudslay's mention in the preface to the work:

Above all, I wish to tender my grateful thanks to Miss Annie Hunter. To students of the inscriptions and sculptures her clever delineation of the carvings will need no further commendation; but I gladly welcome this opportunity of acknowledging the inestimable value of her intelligent and untiring assistance during the eighteen years this work has been in progress.

Since only brief mention of him is made in the text I would also like to pay tribute to the work of Mr A H Anderson, for many years Archaeological Commissioner in British Honduras. He was responsible for guiding many archaeologists in the Maya field and his kindness and co-operation should in themselves be regarded as no small contribution to their studies.

There is here only sufficient space to indicate in the case of each person mentioned the nature and importance of his work; a bibliography is therefore provided for further reading.

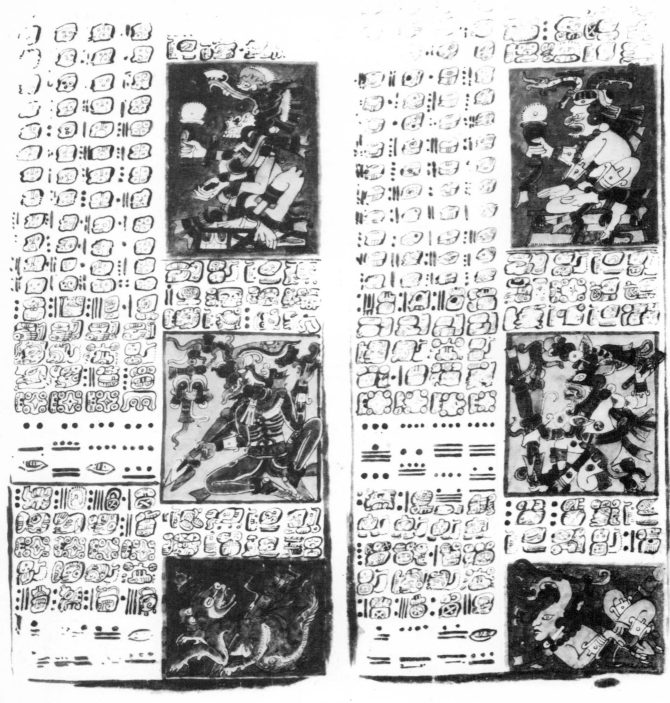

Edward King, Viscount Kingsborough 1795–1837

A Mexican codex, seen by him in the Bodleian Library at Oxford during his student days, inspired Edward King, Viscount Kingsborough, to undertake the enormous task of seeking out and publishing for the first time all such other manuscripts then known. Of ten projected massive volumes, sumptuously bound and illustrated with hand-coloured lithographed plates, only nine were completed between 1831 and Edward King's premature death from jail fever contracted in debtors' prison in 1837. The publication and his considerable support of Frederic Waldeck, self-styled Count, in his expeditionary work searching for ruined sites in Mexico, and possibly inherited family debts, all contributed to the eventual fate of Viscount Kingsborough.

The importance of Kingsborough's *Antiquities of Mexico* is not in the rather confused and rambling text in which it was sought to prove the then not unfashionable theory that the Americas had been peopled by the Lost Tribes of Israel, but in the making available for scholarly study of so much valuable source material. Kingsborough was fortunate, if in nothing else, in the painstaking and astonishingly accurate work of his artist Augustine Aglio. Aglio's rendering of one of the three surviving Maya codices, produced from actual tracings of the *Dresden Codex*, in Volume III of *Antiquities of Mexico*, does indeed contain small errors. But it remains a valued source for some details which have been worn away by subsequent handling of the manuscript.

Plate 1
The only known portrait of Edward King, Viscount Kingsborough. From a photograph in the British Museum.

Plate 2 (right)
Plate from vol. IV of Kingsborough's *Antiquities of Mexico* showing a palace at Palenque, Chiapas.

Plate 3 (left)
A section from the original copy of the *Dresden Codex* made by Augustine Aglio. This was reproduced by Viscount Kingsborough in his *Antiquities of Mexico*, vol. III, 1831.
(British Museum)

Juan Galindo 1802–1839

Juan (born John) Galindo, was the son of the marriage of an English actor, Philemon Galindo, of remote Spanish ancestry, to an Irish actress, Catherine Gough, daughter of a well established but impoverished Anglo-Irish family. John Galindo spent most of his short life as an officer in the service of the army of Central America, but in spite of an active career, found time to write many letters and brief reports of Maya ruins encountered in his travels. Many of these were published in European learned journals, notably the *Bulletins* of the Société de Géographie of Paris. This society honoured him upon several occasions for his work in describing the archaeological sites of Central America, in which there was beginning to be a more and more active interest in the early eighteen-thirties.

A publication by Ian Graham (see bibliography) has assessed the importance of Galindo's contribution to Maya studies at this early period. Galindo noted for example that there was no physical difference between the Indians then living near the ruins of Palenque (a site which he visited in 1831) and the people portrayed in the ancient sculptures there. It was also Galindo who first 'recognised the hieroglyphic writing at Palenque and Copán as a uniquely Maya achievement'.

Probably his most important account is his *Description of the Ruins of Copán*, written in 1834 and accompanied by various drawings of the site and its architecture. Published in 1835, this report played some part in stimulating the American John Lloyd Stephens to undertake his first journey to Central America in 1839.

Colonel Galindo, as he then was, was killed when in retreat from a battle in the interior by a party of Honduran troops.

Plate 4
A miniature painting of Juan Galindo as
a young man.
(Property of Mrs Kathleen Shepard)

Plate 5
Drawing of Stela H at Copán, Honduras,
made by Juan Galindo to accompany
his report on the site to the Société de
Géographie in Paris, 1833.
(Société de Géographie, Paris)

Plate 6
Unpublished lithograph after a drawing
by Juan Galindo of Altar Q, Copán,
Honduras. The lithographer failed to
reverse the drawing and the result is a
mirror image of the original.
(Société de Géographie, Paris)

Plate 7
Altar Q, Copán, Honduras.

John Herbert Caddy 1801–1883

Plate 8
John Herbert Caddy as a young man,
from a painting by Henry Hoppner
Meyer.

Plate 9
A view of the ruins at Palenque, Chiapas,
by Captain J H Caddy, 1840.
(Museum of the American Indian, Heye
Foundation, New York)

John Herbert Caddy, although born in Quebec, was the son of a Kentish
soldier, Captain (later Colonel) John T Caddy, who served in various
military posts in Canada. It was therefore in Amherstburg, Ontario, that
John Herbert received most of his early education and probably developed
the interest in drawing which was to be so important in his later life. In 1815
he came to England to enter the Royal Military Academy and was trained as
an engineer and cannoneer but also had lessons in drawing and water-colour
painting. His early army career included several tours of duty in the West
Indies. In 1838 he was sent as a first lieutenant to the Royal Artillery
Garrison in British Honduras. His diary kept at this period includes both
vivid descriptions of Belize and the surrounding country and an impression,
by contrast, of the somewhat tedious social life surrounding the garrison. The
round of hunts and dinners was interrupted by the decision of the then
Commander-in-Chief, Colonel MacDonald, to send an expedition to the
ruined site of Palenque in which there was considerable interest at this time.
MacDonald had heard that the American diplomat John Lloyd Stephens,
accompanied by the British artist Frederick Catherwood, was intending to
make a journey to the site in order to describe it. MacDonald's intention in
organizing a small expedition seems to have been to forestall them and make
a record of the ruins in the name of the Crown so that it would not appear
that the United States Government was the only one interested in the ruins of
the country.

Patrick Walker, an Englishman holding a bewildering number of official
posts in the settlement, which, Stephens himself said, 'would make the
greatest pluralist among us feel insignificant', was chosen as the leader of the
expedition and Caddy accompanied him since his talent as an artist was well
known.

Walker wrote an official report of what in fact proved to be a successful
expedition both in arriving at Palenque before Stephens and Catherwood and
in providing good drawings of the monuments to accompany the report.
Caddy also kept a diary which gave a lively account of the expedition.
Neither of these was, however, published at the time; the report was buried
in the files of the Colonial Office and, apart from an exhibition of his
drawings which Caddy arranged at the Society of Antiquaries in 1842, no
result of the expedition was placed before the public. Caddy's drawings were

Plate 10
Drawing of a sculptured slab from
Palenque, Chiapas, by Captain J H
Caddy.
(Museum of the American Indian, Heye
Foundation, New York)

neither as extensive nor as detailed as those of Catherwood but they were
among the first serious attempts to record the appearance of a Maya city.
His work was completely overshadowed by the achievements of Stephens and
Catherwood and has remained obscure until the publication of Pendergast's
recent biography upon which this account is based (see bibliography).

Frederick Catherwood 1799–1854

Plate 11
The only known portrait of Frederick
Catherwood. This appears as a detail in
one of the plates in *Views of Ancient
Monuments*, 1844.

In London in 1836 a meeting took place for which all those interested in the study of the Maya can only feel a profound gratitude. John Lloyd Stephens, a well-travelled young American lawyer, met Frederick Catherwood, a London-born architect and artist who had also made journeys to Greece, Turkey and Egypt making drawings of the architectural remains which had come to fascinate him. Stephens at that time was intrigued by the short notices beginning to be published in the early eighteen-thirties of the ruins in the jungles of Central America. In particular a brief account of *The Ruins of Copán in Central America* by Juan Galindo, published in 1835, excited his interest, and in 1839 he set out with Catherwood as artist and companion to find and study the ruins described. The brilliant results of this and their subsequent journeys together during which both often endured much hardship were the first generally available publication of accurate descriptions and illustrations of Maya sites. Stephens's texts, delightful to read for their crispness of style and for the often humorous accounts of the situations encountered, also provide excellent descriptions of the forty-four sites visited, many of which were being reported for the first time. Catherwood's drawings, and the lithographs and engravings afterwards produced from them under his personal supervision, were the first to render faithfully the architectural and decorative style of the Maya monuments. As aids in achieving accuracy in his drawings he employed a camera lucida and, on the second trip to Yucatán, an early daguerreotype camera. The use of such mechanical devices in no way detracted from the atmospheric quality of his final work which so superbly matched Stephens's text.

Of the moral effect of the monuments themselves, standing as they do in the depths of a tropical forest, silent and solemn, strange in design, excellent in sculpture, rich in ornament, different from the works of any other people, their uses and purposes, their whole history so entirely unknown, with hieroglyphs explaining all, but perfectly unintelligible, I shall not pretend to convey any idea. Often the imagination was pained in gazing at them. The tone which pervades the ruins is that of deep solemnity. An imaginative mind might be infected with superstitious feelings. From constantly calling them by that name in our intercourse with the Indians, we regarded these solemn memorials as 'idols' – deified kings and heroes – objects of adoration and ceremonial worship.

The hieroglyphic inscriptions, unintelligible to him as they were, were nevertheless so faithfully drawn by Catherwood that they are recognizable to modern students of the subject. The series of lithographs, made after his drawings, which he published in 1844 in the splendid *Views of ancient monuments in Central America,* also give great aesthetic satisfaction. His results were not always easy to achieve:

I returned to Mr Catherwood, and reported upward of fifty objects to be copied. I found him not so well pleased as I expected with my report. He was standing with his feet in the mud, and was drawing with his gloves on, to protect his hands from the moschetoes. As we feared, the designs were so intricate and complicated, the subjects so entirely new and unintelligible, that he had great difficulty in drawing. He had

Plate 13
Lithograph by Frederick Catherwood of
'A fallen idol at Copán', Honduras; a
plate from *Views of Ancient Monuments*,
1844.

made several attempts, both with the camera lucida and without, but failed to satisfy himself or even me, who was less severe in criticism. The 'idol' seemed to defy his art; two monkeys on a tree on one side appeared to be laughing at him, and I felt discouraged and despondent. In fact, I made up my mind, with a pang of regret, that we must abandon the idea of carrying away any materials for antiquarian speculation, and must be content with having seen them for ourselves. Of that satisfaction nothing could deprive us. We returned to the hut with our interest undiminished, but sadly out of heart as to the result of our labours.

Not the least important result of the labours of Stephens and Catherwood was the interest which they aroused in Alfred Percival Maudslay who was to become one of the greatest students of the Maya.

Alfred Percival Maudslay 1850–1931

Alfred Percival Maudslay, born in 1850, first visited Central America immediately after graduating from Cambridge in 1872. This westward directed 'grand tour', which covered the West Indies, Panama, Guatemala and the United States, was followed, after he had to give up his plans to read medicine, by another voyage to the West Indies, a trip which led almost by accident to his attachment to the Colonial Office and a very active period of service in the South Pacific from 1874 to 1880.

He returned to Guatemala in 1881, in his own words 'to pass the winter in a warm climate'. But the things he saw and the work he did led to this trip being the first of seven which he made to Maya lands between then and 1894. He was accompanied in 1894 by his wife, and together, when they returned home, they pieced together a magnificent book entitled *A Glimpse at Guatemala* which is the only personal record of Maudslay's many expeditions to the country. In this book occurs a simple statement of what he saw his work to be:

I was at Copán for a few days in 1881, and returned there again in 1885, determined to make a more thorough investigation of the ruins, and the result of my work has been published at length in the pages of the *Biologia Centrali-Americana*. . . . It is . . . to the charming pages of Stephens and the beautiful drawings of Catherwood that the world in general is indebted for a knowledge of the wonders of Copán. But delightful as their great book is in every other respect, it does not suffice for a detailed study of Maya art and inscriptions, and my object in returning to the ruins in 1885 was to gather together and publish such a collection of accurate copies of the monuments and inscriptions as would enable scholars to carry on their work of examination and comparison, and to solve some of the many problems of Maya civilization, whilst comfortably seated in their studies at home.

The hardships which Maudslay endured so that scholars should study in comfort are passed over by him in his writing almost without mention. He travelled on his seven trips over the whole of the Maya area at a time when the country was not yet crisscrossed by trails beaten in the search for chicle and none of the modern aids to photography or moulding were available. The major sites he worked on ranged from Chichén Itzá in the north to Copán in the south, from Tikal and Ixkun in the east to Palenque in the west. He seized every opportunity of work – when a franchise negotiated by the Peabody Museum with the Guatemalan Government to excavate

Copán was in danger of lapsing through the death of the leader, Maudslay stepped in and carried on work – and did so always with his own aim in view. He supported himself in his work, did not work 'for' anyone except himself and his goal. At the same time he buried 'self' completely as his words to Charnay, a French archaeologist who had hoped to discover the ruins of Menché (now known as Yaxchilan) and arrived to find Maudslay hard at work, show very well.

. . . there's no reason why you should look so distressed. My having had the start of you was a mere chance, as it would have been mere chance had it been the other way. You need have no fear on my account, for I am only an amateur, travelling for pleasure. With you the case of course is different. But I do not intend to publish anything. Come, I have had a place got ready; and as for the ruins I make them over to you.

Maudslay's photographs, drawings, plans and descriptions were published between 1889 and 1902 as part of *Biologia Centrali-Americana,* edited by Godman and Salvin who subtitled it *Contributions to the Knowledge of the Flora and Fauna of Mexico and Central America.* They had relieved Maudslay of the problem of 'how to make best use of my notes and collections' by adding archaeology to the compass of the massive volumes. The other major fruits of his labours, the moulds which he took in paper and plaster of inscriptions and architectural ornaments in relief (sometimes of great size), the site plans and the collection of negatives have, along with the few original sculptures which he brought to England, become part of the collections of the British Museum. Casts of certain monuments are also in the Cambridge University Museum of Archaeology and Ethnology and the Peabody Museum at Harvard. At the British Museum in 1923 an exhibition was opened in which an entire room was for the first time in the Museum's history devoted to displaying the work of one man still living.

Maudslay's quiet, thorough and determined scholarship resulted in a corpus of material which today is still basic for the student of the Maya. Thomas Athol Joyce wrote in the introduction to his *Guide to the Maudslay Collection of Maya Sculptures (Casts and Originals) from Central America,* prepared in connection with the exhibition, that Maudslay's archaeological volumes provided for the *Biologia Centrali-Americana* were 'not only the one essential textbook for all students of Central American archaeology, but a model of non-controversial exposition of facts'.

Plate 15

The moulding of a large zoomorphic sculpture at Quiriguá, Guatemala. The taking of such moulds and the removal of them to England where casts (now in the British Museum) were prepared from them was one of A P Maudslay's great achievements. It was not always an easy task:

Excavations became filled with water as soon as they were made, and no moulding could be done until a water-tight roof had been made over the monument which was to be moulded. At one time the flood-water covered all but a few feet of ground on which our palm-leaf shanty had been built; everything in camp turned green with mould and mildew, snakes and scorpions became very troublesome, and mosquitos were a continual torment . . .
Towards the end of March the weather became hot and dry and . . . we were able to work on without interruptions until the end of the first week in May. By that time I had secured a complete set of photographs of the monuments, Mr Giuntini, who had worked on steadily . . . had finished a plaster mould of the Great Turtle (a mould which numbered six hundred pieces, and had consumed nearly two tons of plaster) and . . . with the aid of my half-caste companions I had made a paper mould of every inscription in hieroglyphs . . . which we could find in the ruins.

A P Maudslay, *Biologia Centrali-Americana: Archaeology*, vol. II (text), pp. 2–3.

Plate 16
The intricately sculpted monument
known as Zoomorph P from Quiriguá,
Guatemala; a photograph by
A P Maudslay.

Plate 17
Cast from the Maudslay collection
(British Museum) of a relief sculpture at
Palenque, Chiapas, showing a dignitary
seated upon a throne with jaguar heads
being offered an elaborate headdress
trimmed with quetzal plumes.
(British Museum)

Maudslay was awarded honorary doctorates at both Oxford and
Cambridge. I may be excused if I repeat the background to this achievement
with one more quotation from *A Glimpse at Guatemala*:

This was my fourth visit to the ruins of Quirigua. It was here in 1881 I first made
acquaintance with American antiquities. A native from the village guided me to the
site of the ruins, but the undergrowth was so dense that we had some difficulty in
finding any of the monuments, and even when within touch of them, so thickly were
they covered with creepers, ferns, and moss, that it was not easy to distinguish them
from dead tree-trunks. When the creepers and larger plants had been cleared off, the
thick growth of moss still obscured the carving, and as we had come totally un-
prepared to meet this difficulty, some time was occupied in improvising scrubbing-
brushes from bundles of the wiry midribs of palmleaves. The final scrubbing was done
with an ivory-backed hair-brush out of my dressing-bag; and I well remember the
fire of chaff I was subjected to on my return home, when the wreck of that hair-brush
was pounced upon by an old servant who wanted to know 'what Mr Alfred could
have been doing with his hair whilst he was in foreign parts!' We slept only one night
in the forest. . . . It was the unexpected magnificence of the monuments which that day
came into view that led me to devote so many years to securing copies of them, which,
preserved in the museums of Europe and America, are likely to survive the originals.

Plate 19
Drawing of the doorway leading to the
inner chamber of Temple 22, Copán,
Honduras, prepared by Miss Annie
Hunter from Maudslay's photographs.
(British Museum)

Plate 18 (left)
West side of the door leading to the inner
chamber of Temple 22, Copán,
Honduras; a photograph taken by
A P Maudslay.

In 1882 I spent a fortnight among the ruins and cleared enough of the forest to enable
me to take a good set of photographs of the monuments, and returned again in 1883
. . . more thoroughly equipped for the work of exploration, and remained camped in
the ruins for over three months. . . . We commenced work in February . . . until the
first week of May. By that time I had secured a complete set of photographs of each of
the monuments; Mr Giuntini had finished a plaster mould of the great turtle – a
mould of over six hundred pieces . . .

Adela Catherine Breton 1849–1923

Miss Adela Catherine Breton, daughter of Commander William H Breton, RN, was a good linguist and loved to travel. She was also a talented amateur water-colourist as her sketchbooks recording visits to many European countries as well as the Far East and Americas North, Central and South show. Although her interest in archaeology and the arts seems to have been general she became most passionately involved with the antiquities of Mexico. Her obituary notice in *Man* of August 1923 records that she visited Mexico and Central America thirteen times:

In her early expeditions to this region she travelled on horseback over a country which more often than not was roadless, accompanied by only one Indian, who was devoted to her.

Plate 20
Adela Breton with her Mexican guide.
(City Museum, Bristol)

Many of these journeys to Mexico took place between 1894 and 1899. It was Alfred Percival Maudslay who suggested to her the work for which she is chiefly remembered: the recording of mural paintings at the great Maya site of Chichén Itzá in Yucatán, principally the frescoes in the Temple of the Jaguars. Alfred Tozzer, one of the great Mayanists who visited Chichén Itzá, commented: 'This most accurate and painstaking contribution can be understood only by those who saw her laboriously working over the mutilated paintings'. As her diary of these years of work between 1900 and 1904 and again in 1907 records, she was able to correct and augment Maudslay's own superb work at Chichén and to take casts of wooden lintels and door jambs, and colour them, often searching out traces of pigment from the crevices of reliefs to re-create the original.

Her other work of importance was the drawing of the stucco relief mural at the site of Acanceh, Yucatán. Her full-colour version of this elaborate work is now in the City Museum in Bristol where, at her wish, her drawings and sketchbooks and the original colour versions of the Chichén Itzá murals are now housed.

Her own outline description of the work at Chichén, provided for Tozzer (see below), mentions briefly the hardships she endured in procuring these records. I can only conclude with Eric Thompson that 'she must have been a tough, sporting gal. In 1907 she was 57, and there wasn't much comfort in those days'.

Chichén Days

[1900] February 20 to April 1. Nearly died of fever, ticks and hunger. Took the Maudslay plates of sculptured Chamber E and coloured them, the colour being often visible in the hollows of the reliefs, or sunk into the stone where the surface is weathered. It also varies according to the light.

In Temple A (Jaguars) traced and coloured the southern part of west wall frescoes and the piece over the door. Went over carefully the Maudslay plates for corrections and compared the inscription in Casa Colorada with the plate. Made a careful coloured drawing with full details, of the façade of the Monjas Annex. Stayed part of the time in the Akab Tzib. (Visited Uxmal.)

[1901] (To Izamal and Ake) At Chichén January 24 to March 8. Continued copying colours and correcting Maudslay plates. Stayed in Akab Tzib. Pinonillas awful.

Traced and coloured garden scene, east wall of fresco. Worked at improving Maudslay's plates of the lintel and drew the under side. Many visitors and talking, and did little except a coloured drawing of the Door, looking outwards. (Stayed ten days at Uxmal, and visited Labna and Loltun.)

[1902] At Chichén February 4 to May 2. Cleaned west wall of fresco, traced and coloured copy. Also part of east side. Lived in cottage from February 22. Mrs Nuttall and her daughter came on April 2, leaving with Tozzer on the 7th. Traced and coloured fresco in vault of long upper chamber, Monjas, with scaffold. (Visited ruins at Oxkintok near Maxcanu, and Chacmultun.)

[1902–03] At Chichén December 23 to May 4, in same cottage. Used 36 yards of paper 27 inches wide, doing fresco. Photographed North Building of Ball Court and began copying reliefs. Did south wall of fresco, having cleaned out the bats. This wall required much time to clean and study, especially the Sacrifice Scene in the vault. Drew and coloured (two views each) the fifteen caryatid figures found by Bolio in the outer chamber, buried by Dr Le Plongeon who found them standing there, buried in rubbish from fallen roof. They were then taken to the National Museum in Mexico. Also I made out and drew the sculptured table (not all found) that rested on the figures. Photographed them in their right positions, they having had the numbers painted on them by Dr Le Plongeon who photographed them as found (see his 'Queen Moo'). Dr and Mrs Seler came for a few days. She photographed the figures, not in position. (See Dr S's paper in Vienna Congress of Americanists 1908.)

[1904] At Chichén in Temple A, April 9 to June 9. Traced and coloured north wall of fresco, very hard to make out, finished other bits. Worked at North Building reliefs, putting details on enlarged photographs and making drawings of them (see Washington Congress 1915). Copied objects from Cenote, brought by Mr Thompson. Suffered greatly from the huge flying chinches.

[1907] Ten days at Chichén, correcting drawings. (Five weeks at Acanceh, tracing and colouring painted reliefs.)

Thomas William Francis Gann 1867–1938

Plate 22
Thomas Gann with the results of a
non-archaeological pursuit, British
Honduras.

Thomas William Francis Gann, son of William Gann of Whitstable, was
born in Murrish, Ireland, his mother's home. Gann trained in medicine at the
Middlesex Hospital and practised in England before being appointed a
district medical officer in British Honduras in 1894. He quickly developed an
interest in the antiquities of the country and, since his work led him into
remote parts particularly of the Cayo and Corozal districts, made many
discoveries of new groups of ruins and carried out excavations. He is credited
with the discovery of several important sites such as Tzibanche and
Ichpaatún. The important site of Cobá which Gann located in 1926 was
later found to have been visited by Teobert Maler in the eighteen-nineties.
But it was Gann who was responsible for interesting the Carnegie Institution
in the site. This resulted in four expeditions to Cobá from Chichén Itzá where
S G Morley and his staff were working. Eric Thompson participated in these
expeditions and it was at Cobá that he and his wife spent their honeymoon.
Gann also located Lubaantún, the site where the British Museum were to
carry out excavations led by Thomas Athol Joyce in 1926 and 1927 and,
more recently, were to support the work of Norman Hammond in 1970.

Plate 23
An 'eccentric flint' with the profiles of
two figures wearing elaborate head-
dresses. Gann was the first person to
collect information on these curious
examples of Maya stone-working.
(British Museum)

Of his many discoveries, one of the most important was of the at that time
unique mural paintings at the site of Santa Rita which he published in 1901
in his *Mounds in Northern Honduras* for the Bureau of American Ethnology in
Washington. He was also the first person to report on the so called 'eccentric
flints', a form of stone-working characteristic of Maya technology. His
papers in scientific periodicals were numerous, but he published in addition
six eminently readable popular volumes describing his life and experiences in
British Honduras which, like his various articles for the *Illustrated London
News* and his talks for the BBC, did much to focus the attention of the public
upon the Maya civilization of which little was generally known at the time.

When he retired in 1923 he was principal medical officer in British
Honduras and had occasionally been called to take on the duties of acting
district commissioner. Although he had already established his interest in the
Maya, he was from this time able to devote himself more fully to the study of
their culture. From 1919 until his death in 1938 he was lecturer in Central
American Archaeology at the University of Liverpool, the first person ever to
hold such a position in England. The British Museum has several important
collections of Maya material given and bequeathed by Gann, including his
famous collection of jade carvings. He also deposited with the University of
Liverpool a fine Maya archaeological collection now in the City of Liverpool
Public Museums.

The somewhat unkind and patronising description of Gann by the
journalist Gregory Mason as 'a picturesque old Britisher who was skinny and
rather crabbed but likeable' is a sadly inadequate one. T A Joyce and Sylvanus
Morley both appreciated Gann and Eric Thompson found him 'generous,
likeable and with a pawky sense of humour' whilst recalling also that he had

. . . a rotten temper. I remember walking with him along an old truck pass (a road cut
in forest to get out mahogany). We came to a steep and muddy hill. Old Gann
stopped about a third of the way up and cussed the hill for what seemed like about
ten minutes. By the time he stopped he had no breath left to climb the hill.

He remains a difficult person to assess. Thompson admits that Gann would
'spin a good yarn which would grow a bit like a fisherman's catch' and this
perhaps helps to explain the rather sensational approach of his popular books.
In his book *Maya Cities*, after telling how he set off with a 'Chief's Son' in

search of an idol never before seen by white men (it is true that Gann was often in this position – the first white man to see a Maya ruin), he describes arriving at a small temple with a single low doorway on the south side:

On looking through the doorway into the cool, dark interior of the little temple, a curious sight met our eyes, which made us start back momentarily in surprise. Sitting upon the highest of three small terraces, forming a platform at the back of the temple, and staring straight out through the door, between half-closed lids, as it had stared unblinkingly for more than five hundred years, was the figure of an idol ... This was probably a unique find, as I doubt if, throughout the whole of Yucatán, there exists today a temple, perfect in itself, with the unaltered figure of the god within it, practically in the same state and the same position as he was left in by his worshippers.

At the same site of Tuluum where the above took place Gann visited the father of his guide, the local *cacique*, or chief, of the Santa Cruz Indians whose name was Canul. He reports the following conversation when

à propos of nothing in particular, he suddenly asked me the extraordinary question: 'Does your English King talk with God?'
I was completely flabbergasted, and could only answer:
'I really don't know, as I have never had the honour of conversation with the King. Why do you ask?'
'But,' he said, 'isn't the King a son of La Reina Victoria?'
'No,' said I; 'he is her grandson.'
'Ah,' returned Canul, 'that may account for it. We always heard that La Reina Victoria was the greatest and best woman in the world, and that she actually talked with God, and I thought the gift might have come down to her son; but her grandson – that would be too much to expect.'

It was Gann's contact with the Indians, his invaluable knowledge of British Honduras, a country in which travel was extremely difficult and sometimes dangerous, and his determination in the face of all obstacles to follow up information about Maya remains in isolated regions of the country, which make him sometimes seem ubiquitous when one reads about exploration in Maya lands around the turn of the century. He was an invaluable companion to many of the archaeologists who came to work there, and he himself made no small contribution in stimulating archaeological work in British Honduras.

Plate 24
Stucco figure from a temple at Tuluum, Yucatán, collected by Thomas Gann. (British Museum)

Plate 25
Part of a reconstructed drawing of a
fresco at the site of Santa Rita, British
Honduras, made by Thomas Gann. It
shows the western half of the north wall
of Mound 1.

Note on the teaching of American archaeology in England
Thomas Gann was Lecturer in the Archaeology of Central America at the University
of Liverpool between 1919 and 1938. How regularly he lectured, and whether his
students were examined, I do not know. Perhaps at the time lack of interest made it
difficult for him to find students at all. Since that time there has been no university
teaching offered in the field of American archaeology which could lead to being
examined in it, since the lectures given by teachers such as T A Joyce and Dr Geoffrey
Bushnell have always been only a small part of general courses in archaeology. In
1967 the University of London appointed Dr Warwick Bray as Lecturer in Latin
American Archaeology. His course at the Institute of Archaeology is available to
undergraduates and he has successfully steered several students through doctoral
theses on American archaeological subjects and has several students with work in
progress.

Thomas Athol Joyce 1879–1942

Thomas Athol Joyce joined the staff of the British Museum in 1902 as an Oxford graduate in Classics. The ethnographical collections were at that time a part of the Department of British and Mediaeval Antiquities under the Keepership of Charles Hercules Read. They became Joyce's particular concern; and work on the *Handbook to the Ethnographical Collections*, started by Ormonde Maddock Dalton, was continued by Joyce from 1902 until its publication in 1910. It must have been during those years that he acquired his wide range of knowledge and interests in all aspects of anthropology. The *Handbook* was followed by the short *Guide to American Antiquities* in 1912. Joyce had also reorganized the Ancient American section of the gallery and by this date had the reputation of being an authority on this subject. Three works on American archaeology published outside the Museum, *South American Archaeology* (1912), *Mexican Archaeology* (1914) and *Central American and West Indian Archaeology* (1916) attest to his position as one of the leading writers in this field.

Plate 26
Captain Thomas Athol Joyce at the site of Lubaantún British Honduras.

Plate 27
Pottery figurine of a woman grinding maize; she carries a child on her back. This is an example of the many figurines from the Lubaantún site which give a unique view of the everyday life of the Maya. It was excavated by the British Museum expedition to British Honduras in 1927.
(British Museum)

Plate 28
Stone mask from Mound II at Pusilhá
excavated by the British Museum
expedition to British Honduras in 1928.
5¼in (13·3cm)
(British Museum)

Plate 29
A specimen of fine polychrome painted
pottery from Pusilhá, British Honduras,
excavated by the British Museum
expedition in 1929.
(British Museum)

It was largely Joyce's efforts which secured the transfer of the magnificent collection of casts, sculptures and photographs made by Alfred Maudslay from the cellars of the Victoria and Albert Museum where they had lain for thirty years. Joyce arranged an exhibition of this material in what came to be called the Maudslay Room and wrote the *Guide to the Maudslay Collection of Casts and Sculptures* which appeared in 1923. Although this came some time after the end of Maudslay's fieldwork in the Maya area in 1894, it was the first exhibition to pay tribute to him and his great work.

Joyce himself embarked upon a series of field expeditions to British Honduras between 1926 and 1931, four of which he led himself, on special leave from his duties for four months in each case. The results of this work were published in the *Journal* of the Royal Anthropological Institute, and the excavated material forms one of the British Museum's most important basic collections of Maya material, having been brought here with the consent and help of the government of British Honduras. For the 1927 season one of the members of the expedition party was J Eric S Thompson, then at the beginning of his career as a student of the Maya.

By this time Joyce was Deputy Keeper in charge of what had become the Sub-Department of Ethnography. In 1932 Adrian Digby joined the staff and worked with Joyce until the latter retired in 1938 due to ill health. It was presumably this association which interested Digby in American antiquities.

A former Keeper, H J Braunholtz, wrote the following of Joyce in a history of the Department of Ethnography published in the *British Museum Quarterly* in 1953 (and reprinted in *Sir Hans Sloane and Ethnography*, exhibition handbook, 1970):

He thoroughly enjoyed introducing novices to the treasures under his charge and would go to much trouble to engage their interest. By disposition he was sociable and cheerful. Indeed the spirited sounds of whistling and song, which might sometimes be heard emanating from his corner of the room, exasperated the austerer temper of at least one of his older colleagues, who regarded such unbridled manifestations of gaiety in the study as improper, if not positively demoralising . . . One of the writer's earliest impressions of him was as he lay stretched full length on the floor poring over the unwieldy volumes of Kingsborough's *Mexican Antiquities*, which were far too large to be opened on any of the desks or tables in the study.

John Eric Sidney Thompson b. 1898

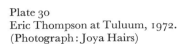

Plate 30
Eric Thompson at Tuluum, 1972.
(Photograph: Joya Hairs)

When Eric Thompson entered the field of Maya archaeology there was no formal teaching available in the subject anywhere in England. He therefore, having studied anthropology under 'that great teacher Alfred Haddon' at Cambridge, taught himself, and in particular devised a simple method of learning Maya glyphs. By drawing them all, placing them in a hat and picking them out at random until he could recognise every variant form of each glyph without looking at the name written on the back, Eric Thompson made himself expert in reading inscriptions. In 1925 he wrote to Dr Sylvanus G Morley, head of the Chichén Itzá archaeological project of the Carnegie Institution of Washington, asking him for a job.

My chief asset, the ability to read and compute Maya hieroglyphic dates, was one I knew would appeal to Morley, whose whole life had been devoted to that subject; students of Maya glyphs were as scarce as hen's teeth.

This was a characteristically energetic launching into a career which is, as
yet, happily not at end. In his autobiographical book, *Maya Archaeologist*,
Eric Thompson has described life in those early days of Maya archaeology.
His literary style well suits the vivid and varied nature of the life. He
describes himself as having the fortune to belong

– although only by the skin of my teeth – to the last generation of archaeologists who
were able to have extended interests. Now, with the enormous increase of knowledge,
fields of specialisation are so narrow that archaeologists are in danger of becoming
technicians.

Those familiar with his publications on the Maya, too numerous to list here,
are grateful to Eric Thompson's sense of responsibility towards the travellers
or readers interested in Maya civilization who

return from their journeys, physical or mental, curiously unsatisfied. They have been
deeply impressed by great archaeological wonders and magnificent sculptures erected
in this remote area by a strange people which unaccountably has disappeared from
the stage of history.

No-one has done so much to clothe with flesh the bare bones of archaeological
fact as Eric Thompson. Most of his working life before retirement was spent
in the United States and Latin America and he has been many times
honoured for his achievements in both these places. His work since retirement
in England has been no less prolific. A recent BBC television film (produced
for the *Chronicle* programme) made a wider British public aware of one of their
most eminent scholars and remarkable men. Eric Thompson has elsewhere
long been recognised as a foremost authority on Maya hieroglyphic writing.
In his work on the glyphs he makes full use of his vast knowledge of archaeological and historical source material and also his equally important knowledge
of and friendship with the Maya of the present day and recent past.

In the early days of his career as a field archaeologist Eric Thompson
worked with T A Joyce at the site of Lubaantún, British Honduras. This
association with the activities of the British Museum has fortunately
continued, although intermittently, ever since. The Museum received a share
of the material resulting from his important excavations in the Cayo district
in the nineteen-thirties carried out for the Field Museum of Natural History
in Chicago when he was assistant curator of Central and South American

archaeology there. He has also generously helped to fill gaps in the Department of Ethnography's archaeological and ethnographical collections from the Americas. Most recently he has written for the British Museum a book, *Maya Hieroglyphs without Tears* (1972) which will guide the now numerous interested students as painlessly as possible into the enormously complex subject of Maya hieroglyphic decipherment.

Most especially we have to thank Eric Thompson now for the time and trouble he always takes to answer questions and offer advice on all things Maya. I can only echo the toast once offered to him when he

spent New Year's Eve in the hut of my old friend Benito, the Rockefeller of Lubaantún. It was my birthday so we celebrated. After several toasts and much rum-swigging, Benito gave a toast I am unlikely to forget. With a slight lurch he raised his glass and called to the company, 'Vivan Dios y Meester Tonson', Long live God and Mister Thompson.

Plate 32
Eric Thompson making notes on a
hieroglyphic inscription at Palenque.

Adrian Digby b. 1909

Plate 33
Adrian Digby (left) and A H Anderson, Archaeological Commissioner for British Honduras, with their workmen at the Las Cuevas site in 1957.

Plate 34
Part of the excavations inside the cave at the Las Cuevas site showing *in situ* a potstand made from a fragment of a broken urn. This had originally supported a funerary vessel filled with bone ash, the sherds of which were also found in the excavation. When the upper vessel was smashed by earth movement, the bone ash fell through into the potstand.

Adrian Digby became a member of the staff of the British Museum when he joined what was then the Sub-Department of Ethnography as an Assistant Keeper in 1932 during the Deputy Keepership of T A Joyce. The post required of him responsibility for the Museum's collections of both archaeology and ethnography from the whole of the Americas. But on the two occasions when he had the opportunity to work in the field, Adrian Digby went to the Maya area.

The previous occasion on which the British Museum had financed field work in the Americas had been the five seasons of excavation in British Honduras conducted by Joyce in 1926–31. In 1957 Adrian Digby, accompanied by Mr A H Anderson, the Archaeological Commissioner for British Honduras, carried out excavations at the site of Las Cuevas in the Cayo district of British Honduras. Anderson had visited the Las Cuevas site in 1938 and made a brief report on it to the Americanists' Congress in 1952:

There is a connecting chain of at least five limestone caves all containing sherds, and some whole pottery. The outer cave is intersected by a subterranean stream, the inner bank of which is artificially built up: test holes produced both sherds and some whole pottery. Behind this is an area marked off into small, irregularly shaped plots by stones placed on end. The opening leading into the second cave is built up with masonry to form a small doorway. There are mounds round the area of the caves.

The expedition was supported by the British Academy as well as the British Museum. It was gravely hampered at the outset by severe flooding which reduced the time they were able to spend on the site from three months to seven weeks. And the site – a fair-sized complex of buildings never before investigated and covered in dense jungle, and a huge cave divided by walls and strewn with pots and sherds at all depths – was far from being an easy one to work on. Nevertheless, in the short time left Digby carried out sufficient excavation and recorded enough information to speculate about the function of the cave and the pottery within it in lectures and an article in the *Illustrated London News*. It is a matter for regret that the pressures of the Keepership of the Department, a post which he held from 1953 until his retirement in 1969, did not allow him to follow up what could be no more than a preliminary investigation. The proper study of sites so difficult of access and so elusive of explanation as those of a culture of which many aspects are still mysterious requires an ordered, systematic approach only possible in the field over several seasons, preferably in consecutive years.

Plate 35
A photograph of a façade from the
building known as Las Monjas at the
site of Uxmal, Yucatán, taken by
Adrian Digby.

In 1955 appeared *Ancient American Pottery* which Adrian Digby wrote
jointly with Dr G H S Bushnell; and he has also published articles in
journals and in Chambers's *Encyclopaedia*. In 1964 he wrote a booklet with the
title *Maya Jades* which was published by the British Museum and of which a
second edition has been published (1972). This illustrates a large number of
fine specimens in the collections of the Department of Ethnography. The
text presents some interesting theories concerning the technology of jade
carving and is an interesting popular introduction to an important group
of objects.

In the year before his retirement, Adrian Digby travelled to Mexico, this
time for a period of six months, to photograph the architectural remains at
various archaeological sites, many of them in the Maya area. This was to
provide a study collection of photographic material which was very much
needed in the Department. For all the long tradition of British contact with
Maya lands, documentary material of this kind is still hard to come by in
England and future students will benefit greatly from this work.

Ian Graham b. 1923

Plate 36
Ian Graham photographing Structure 5,
Yaxchilan, Guatemala.

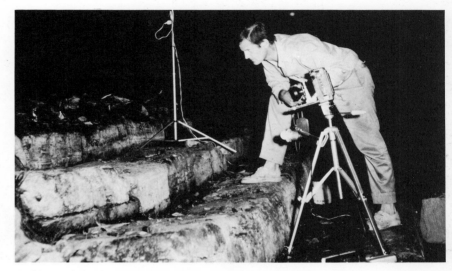

In his work in the Maya area Ian Graham encounters possibly more
excitement and greater tragedy than most archaeologists. Since 1959 he has
worked in the rain forests of the Petén in Guatemala, locating and recording
Maya sites in the vast areas of now uninhabited jungle. He has paid
particular attention to monuments with hieroglyphic inscriptions. The
excitement of his work comes in the finding of sites (or the locating of sites
which, although recorded, have become 'lost' again beneath the forest
growth), often after journeys no less arduous, uncomfortable and fraught
with danger than those of the first European explorers in the Maya area.
And then the 'mixed feelings of awe and excitement that well up at the first
sight of a stela still standing after a thousand years of hazard in the forest'.

The tragedy consists in finding that sometimes looters have been there
before him – perhaps not very long before. In 1971 a Guatemalan assistant
travelling with him was shot dead by looters disturbed in their work at a site
which Graham was visiting. The looting of archaeological sites is now
tragically a very profitable, and therefore booming, business. The techniques
of the robbers vary in their degree of sophistication. Monuments, often
inscribed stelae, are sawn up and removed from Guatemala by helicopter;

Plate 37
Stela 8, Dos Pilas, Guatemala (about AD 730).
The photograph by Ian Graham shows the stela in a mutilated state with the upper part of the inscriptions (at left) removed by looters. The Initial Series glyph and a further group of four glyphs have been neatly sawn off.

they are also sometimes smashed into pieces of convenient size and carried out from the forest on mules. All are destined to feed the underground art markets of the world. The history of pieces thus removed from their contexts is lost and even their place of origin is sometimes knowingly suppressed. They then appear in museum or private collections as works of art but their further potential as keys to the still in so many ways unknown Maya can probably never be realized.

As director of a project to prepare and publish a corpus of all known Maya inscriptions it is of particular urgency to Ian Graham to try to stay one step ahead of the looters. They work in the remote areas as he does, where control of their activities is difficult, usually impossible. If he can record the position of the sculptures and photograph, draw or take moulds of the inscribed areas then something has been saved. After working throughout the dry

Plate 38
Drawing of the inscription from Stela 11,
Machaquila, Guatemala, by
Ian Graham.

season each year in Guatemala, Ian Graham returns to the Peabody Museum at Harvard, where he is a Research Fellow, to write up and make finished drawings of the material collected.

Ian Graham's most important publication to date has been his *Archaeological Explorations in El Peten, Guatemala* in which the excellent photographs and superb drawings made from them demonstrate the success of special techniques which he has evolved for work under extremely difficult conditions. In some cases this is painstaking work. Writing of a stela at the site of Naranjo, Guatemala, on which the inscription can only faintly be seen, Graham noted that

when examined by the diffuse light that filters through the forest canopy, the text incised at the back of this stela is scarcely noticeable; both Maler and Morley refer to it as eroded beyond hope of recovery. Yet by careful lighting, a large amount of detail can be captured photographically.

The drawing he made of this stela

was based on a photograph taken of the stela when the glyphs had been emphasised with water-soluble ink. This had been applied at night to each faint line as it showed up under a hand lamp constantly moved about for best effect . . . by this technique more was recovered than shows in the photograph.

Graham's finished drawings are also based on freehand sketches which incorporate 'all that can be made out of the often indistinct design when illuminated at various angles, using light from a gasoline-driven generator.'

The meticulous accuracy and deep understanding which the completed drawings reflect have earned for Ian Graham the respect and appreciation of the greatest scholars in this field. The manner in which he works can be said most closely to resemble that of the great Alfred Maudslay.

In addition to his contributions as a field archaeologist, Ian Graham has an interest in the history of Maya studies. His article, *Juan Galindo, enthusiast* has already been mentioned. In 1971 he prepared a successful exhibition shown in New York with the title 'The Art of Maya Hieroglyphic Writing' for which he also wrote the catalogue. This was a survey of the study of Maya hieroglyphs from the time of the Conquest to the present day and helped to make a wide public aware of the fascination of this study and the enormous amount of work still to be done.

Norman Hammond b. 1944

Plate 39
Norman Hammond at Lubaantún,
British Honduras, 1970.

Plate 40
Plan of Lubaantún, British Honduras,
made by members of Norman
Hammond's expedition in 1970.

Norman Hammond is at present the only British archaeologist working in
the Maya area while continuing to be based in England. He entered the
field of American archaeology in 1967 when he was appointed the first
Research Fellow in that subject at the Centre of Latin American Studies at
the University of Cambridge. He had previously carried out fieldwork in
North Africa and Afghanistan. In 1968 he worked as an assistant on the
staff of the Peabody Museum (Harvard) excavations at the Maya site of
Seibal in Guatemala.

In 1970, as part of the programme of research for his doctoral thesis,
Hammond organised a season of fieldwork at the site of Lubaantún, British
Honduras. This was carried out with the co-operation of the Government of
Belize (British Honduras) and the financial support of the Cambridge
University Museum of Archaeology and Ethnology, the Peabody Museum,
the British Museum, the Pitt Rivers Museum (Oxford), the British Academy
and the Wenner-Gren Foundation.

Lubaantún had been explored by Thomas Gann in 1903 and again in
1924–5, and it was he who encouraged Captain T A Joyce of the British
Museum to work at this site which he did in 1926–7 as part of the first and
only series of field excavations in American archaeology upon which the
British Museum has ever embarked. Some support for Joyce's work came
from the Maya Exploration Fund, now sadly defunct, which made a public
appeal for money, never successful on the right scale, but well supported by
eminent men of the day interested in archaeology and anthropology; this,
with the additional sums granted by the British Museum, enabled Joyce to
organize six successive field projects.

The excavations of Joyce and his colleagues at Lubaantún had not entirely
explained features of the site which interested Norman Hammond. In
accordance with modern practice his approach to the archaeology of
Lubaantún was on an interdisciplinary basis and set out to accumulate
data on the site and its surrounding area to assist in the interpretation of the
archaeological finds:

The project's programme was in three parts: the first was to make an accurate large-
scale plan of the ceremonial centre of Lubaantún, supplemented by a map of part of
the settlement around it; the second to establish by means of excavation the period for
which the site had been occupied, the way in which it had grown, and the develop-

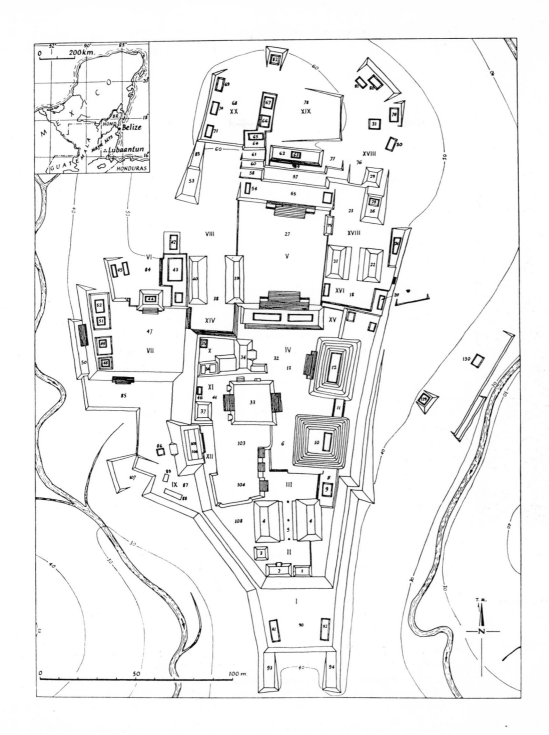

ment of architectural styles; the third was to assess the range of natural resources available to the ancient inhabitants of Lubaantún, to see how they exploited them and also what factors had induced them to settle in this precise spot. The survey included geology, soil-classification, and cataloguing of plant species, and was augmented by investigation of the present local hunting practices and use of forest products for housing, food, domestic equipment, medicine and religious observances.

Norman Hammond, *Lubaantún 1926–70: the British Museum in British Honduras*, 1972

Lubaantún had idiosyncratic 'stepped perpendicular' architecture, but lacked masonry buildings on top of the stone-faced pyramids and also lacked the plain or carved stone monuments called stelae, although from its size it was clearly a centre of major importance. The 1970 excavations showed that Lubaantún was even more unusual than had been thought, having been established in virgin territory as late as the eighth century AD (whereas comparable sites in Guatemala have been found to go back to 800 BC, 1600 years earlier) and abandoned after less than a century and a half. The excavations demonstrated how a Maya centre had grown through time, by the successive accumulation of massive rubble-filled hill-platforms around a natural ridge. At the same time a sample area of one square kilometre around the site was mapped and the nature of the settlement of Lubaantún established. The houses were grouped on the tops of knolls, to catch the wind and light and avoid flooding during the torrential downpours of the wet season (Lubaantún has over thirteen feet of rain a year), and the maximum population density if they were all occupied at once is estimated at 1,000 per square mile. Each house group was surrounded by steep slopes which could be used for growing maize and beans, the staple diet of the Maya. A programme of ecological survey showed that Lubaantún was sited in the middle of good maize and cacao lands, close to hunting and plant-gathering territories and with easy access down the Rio Grande to the Caribbean. Thus the project placed a small regional centre in its ecological and economic context, answering in detail the question of why Lubaantún had been established in this spot; the centre was related to its 'realm', and this realm placed in the total context of the Classic Maya world.

In addition to his history of archaeology at Lubaantún published by the British Museum and quoted above, Norman Hammond is preparing a monograph on the characteristic figurines from the site which illustrate in a

unique way the everyday life of the Maya. This will also be published by the British Museum and will expand the coverage already given to this interesting subject by T A Joyce in his Presidential Address to the Royal Anthropological Institute for 1933 on *Pottery Whistle-Figurines of Lubaantún*.

A further season of fieldwork in British Honduras under the leadership of Norman Hammond and sponsored by the Trustees of the British Museum is in preparation. This will be carried out in the Corozal region, northern British Honduras, commencing early in 1973. It is to be hoped that further money and resources can be found in future years to enable Norman Hammond and other students to develop and expand research on the Maya in England. There is a tradition of outstanding contributions upon which to build, the importance of which can only be suggested briefly within the scope of this booklet.

Plate 41
Pottery figurine from Lubaantún showing the head of a ballplayer in profile. He wears the characteristic helmet surmounted by a crest of feathers. Excavated by Norman Hammond in 1970.

Bibliography

Braunholtz, H J, 'History of Ethnography in the museum after 1753 (part II)' in *British Museum Quarterly*, xviii, 4 (1953) (reprinted in *Sir Hans Sloane and Ethnography*, 1970)

Breton, Adela C, 'Archaeology in Mexico', in *Man*, 17, 1908, pp. 34–7

Breton, Adela C, 'The ancient frescoes at Chichén Itzá' in *Journal of the British Association*, Section H (1911)

Breton, Adela C, 'Preliminary study of the North Building (Chamber C), Great Ball Court, Chichén Itzá' in *Proceedings of the Nineteenth International Congress of Americanists* (Washington 1917)

Breton, Adela C (artist), drawings in Eduard Seler, *Die Stuckfassade von Acanceh in Yucatán* (Berlin 1911)

Carmichael, Captain John, 'On the ruined cities of Central America' in *Report of the British Association* (1870)

Catherwood, Frederick, *Views of ancient monuments in Central America, Chiapas, and Yucatan* (New York 1844)

Coe, Michael D, *The Maya* (London 1966)

Digby, Adrian, *Maya Jades* (London 1964, second edition 1972)

Digby, Adrian and G H S Bushnell, *Ancient American Pottery* (London 1955)

Digby, Adrian, article in *Illustrated London News* (15 February 1958)

Gann, Thomas, 'Mounds in Northern Honduras' in *Nineteenth Annual Report of the Bureau of American Ethnology* (Washington 1901)

Gann, Thomas, *In an unknown land* (London 1924)

Gann, Thomas, *Mystery cities* (London 1925)

Gann, Thomas, *Ancient cities and modern tribes: explorations and ventures in Maya lands* (London 1926)

Gann, Thomas, *Maya cities* (London 1927)

Gann, Thomas, *Discoveries and adventures in Central America* (London 1928)

Gann, Thomas and J Eric S Thompson, *The history of the Mayas from the earliest time to the present day* (New York 1931)

Gann, Thomas, *Glories of the Maya* (London 1938)

Gann: a full bibliography of the works of Thomas Gann was prepared by J Eric S Thompson and is published in *Boletín Bibliográfico de Antropología Americana*, iv (Mexico 1940)

Graham, Ian, 'Juan Galindo, enthusiast', *Estudios de Cultura Maya*, iii (Mexico 1963)

Graham, Ian, *Archaeological explorations in El Petén, Guatemala* (New Orleans 1967)

Graham, Ian, *The art of Maya hieroglyphic writing*, catalogue of an exhibition in the art gallery of the Center for Inter-American Relations (New York 1971)

Hagen, Victor Wolfgang von, *Maya explorer: John Lloyd Stephens and the lost cities of Central America and Yucatán* (Norman 1947)

Hagen, Victor Wolfgang von, *Frederick Catherwood architect* (New York 1950)

Hammond, Norman, 'Excavations at Lubaantún 1970', *Antiquity* xliv, pp. 216–23 (Cambridge 1970)

Hammond, Norman, *Lubaantún 1926–70: The British Museum in British Honduras* (London 1972)

Hammond, Norman, 'Locational models and the site of Lubaantún: a Classic Maya centre', *Models in Archaeology*, ed. D L Clarke, pp. 757–800 (London)

Hammond, Norman, articles in *Illustrated London News* (6 and 20 January 1971)

Joyce, T A, *Mexican archaeology* (London 1914)

Joyce, T A, *Guide to the Maudslay collection of Maya sculptures (casts and originals) from Central America* (London 1922, 1938)

Joyce, T A, *Maya and Mexican art* (London 1927)

Joyce, T A, 'The pottery whistle-figurines of Lubaantún', Presidential Address, *Journal of the Royal Anthropological Institute*, lxiii (London 1933)

Joyce, T A, and others: the reports on the British Museum expeditions to British Honduras in 1926–30 were published yearly in the *Journal of the Royal Anthropological Institute*. Remaining offprints of these reports were sold by the British Museum. The individual titles and their authors are as follow

  Joyce, 'Report on the investigations at Lubaantún . . . 1926'
  Joyce, Cooper Clark and Thompson, 'Report on the British Museum expedition to British Honduras, 1927'
  Joyce, Gann, Gruning and Long, ditto, 1928
  Joyce, ditto, 1929
  Gruning, ditto, 1930

Joyce: a full bibliography of the publications of Thomas Athol Joyce was prepared by J Eric S Thompson and published in *Boletín Bibliográfico de Antropología Americana*, xiii (2) (Mexico 1950)

Kingsborough, Edward King, Lord, *Antiquities of Mexico: comprising facsimiles of ancient Mexican paintings and hieroglyphs*, 9 volumes (London 1831–1848)

Maudslay, Alfred Percival, *Biologia Centrali-Americana: Archaeology*, 4 volumes (London 1889–1902)

Maudslay, Alfred Percival, *Life in the Pacific fifty years ago* (London 1930)

Maudslay, Anne Cary and Alfred Percival, *A glimpse at Guatemala* (London 1899)

Pendergast, David M, *Palenque: the Walker-Caddy expedition to the ancient Maya city, 1839–1840* (Norman 1967)

Robertson, D, *Mexican manuscript painting of the early colonial period (the metropolitan schools)* (New Haven 1959)

Stephens, John Lloyd, *Incidents of travel in Central America, Chiapas and Yucatan* (London 1841)

Stephens, John Lloyd, *Incidents of travel in Yucatan* (New York 1843)

Thompson, J Eric S, *Archaeological investigations in the southern Cayo district, British Honduras* (Chicago 1931)

Thompson, J Eric S, *Maya hieroglyphic writing: an introduction* (Washington 1950; Norman 1960)

Thompson, J Eric S (ed.), *Thomas Gage's travels in the New World* (Norman 1962)

Thompson, J Eric S, *Maya archaeologist* (Norman 1963)

Thompson, J Eric S, *The rise and fall of Maya civilisation* (Norman 1966)

Thompson, J Eric S, *Maya history and religion* (Norman 1970)

Thompson, J Eric S, *Maya hieroglyphs without tears* (London 1972)

Tozzer, Alfred Marston, 'Alfred Percival Maudslay', in *American Anthropologist*, **33**, 3 (1931)

Tozzer, Alfred Marston, *Chichén Itzá and its cenote of sacrifice*, Peabody Museum of Archaeology and Ethnology Memoirs 11–12 (Cambridge Massachusetts 1957)

Waldeck, Jean Frédéric de, *Voyage pittoresque et archéologique dans la province d'Yucatan (Amérique Centrale) pendant les années 1834 et 1836* (Paris 1838)

Wauchope, Robert, *They found buried cities* (Chicago and London 1965)